Silent Dreams

Marissa Alexa McCool

For media or questions, contact
patorrez@patorrez.com

To: Aiden, Jeanne, Amy, Nathanial, Michael, Kieran
LaLa, Aaron, Monk, Eli, Anna, Tom, Cecil
Thomas, Andrew, Dan, Matthew, Callie, Ari

Thank you for helping me find my voice

Introduction

Stop: I know what you're thinking. "Another one, Ris? Really? Another book?" Yes.

While this one will not delay the release of *Voice in the Dark* (coming soon), this is different. These are a series of poems and essays I wrote in my first few months of living openly as a transwoman, of being myself, and for which some of the time, I received quite a bit of negative feedback from the supposed ally community.

But this is a real story. A story of how I got to where I am, and the journey I had to take to get there. There's not much I can add to that, save for the fact that there's always someone waiting to tell me that I'm wrong, or that I didn't have the experience I had. It's far easier to leave the status quo the way it is than it is to change something. Those who are fine with oppression take the side of the oppressor.

I hope you enjoy these works, and I hope you like the novel coming out soon, featuring Dan Arel, Noah Lugeons, Karen Garst, and many others. For now, here's some of my work since I came out.

Thank you.

Reflections on Pulse

It's been almost a year since 49 members of our community were needlessly and heartlessly murdered. That event was the impetus of my transition. I read a letter that I'd written "anonymously" on the Inciting Incident episode where we talked about it, and it was only a month later that I secretly went on hormones.

That event made me want to be loud. That event made me want to yell. That event made me want to be visible. No matter what kind of danger it puts me in, because this kinda shit needs to stop, and the douchebros and ignoramuses are not helping.

I know you think it's totes hilarious to make the "only two genders" joke, like we've heard it for the first time, but you're the ones who get offended when someone other than you exists, or walks down the street holding hands with another transwoman.

I know you think we made all this up and that makes us crazy, but I think that makes you an ableist bigot with an awful lot of lonely nights spent trolling a noncis space on Facebook because you literally have nothing else to do.

I'm tired of having to fight for our humanity. I'm tired of having to fight to be acknowledged as people. I'm tired of having courts decide that crimes against us aren't hate crimes because Jesus said we shouldn't be that way or something. Can't we charge them with hate crimes by making being ourselves even more dangerous than it already is?

I'm tired of having to ask someone to go to the bathroom with me. I'm tired of wondering if the next person to give me the stink eye has a gun. I'm tired of wondering if someone who sees my husband and I together is going to say something in front of my kids. I'm tired of worrying about every single queer and visible friend I have and their safety, because supposed followers of the God who said "love everyone" and those who clamor for the sanctity of life and all lives mattering also love to tell us that that loving God took 49 members of our community away in senseless violence because love, or because we're all perverts, or because we are the army of darkness, or because purple makes them get flashbacks over titty twisters... Whatever it is, I don't fucking care, and I'm sick of having to justify our community's humanity daily to the crowd that is so willing to openly disregard experts in order to continue being an ignorant asshole.

I've been attacked recently by both strangers and people I considered friends. I've been attacked because I have the nerve to stand up for myself when someone shouts a shitty opinion at me. I've been attacked for thinking I know myself better than some stranger who is sure that he knows what gender really is. I've been attacked for having a visible show that isn't about what's going on in their lives, but instead focuses on our own community cause, you know, we've taken over everything and that's all it is anymore. Look at all our fucking representation, guys. We really should get the cis straight white guys a chance once in a while, right?

Today, I sat and stared at messages. Countless messages, handwritten, on posters, on sidewalks, on rocks... I saw 49 names inscribed, including my own last name as second on the list. I imagined the sounds of that night; the visions, the terror, the fear... And I thought about every single person I heard mocking that event, or using it to promote hatred, or to make a shitty joke because special snowflakes can't take their sense of humor because we don't find jokes about the murder of our already-vulnerable community to be fucking funny!

I speak out for them, not the ones who can't handle everything not being about them. I speak out for the chosen queer family I have, and the ones I don't know, who have to live day to day, wondering if they're going to be safe or if their dad is going to acknowledge their existence or if they're going to have a place to live because of who they are. I became an activist because I am sick and fucking tired of all lives mattering until they found out they might be queer. I'm sick and fucking tired of life being sacred unless Jesus cries when queers kiss. I'm sick and fucking tired of knowledge being power, unless it affirms what we already know about our sexuality and gender, and then some fucking idiot named Todd knows better cause he got a C in eighth grade biology, and that's pretty much the same thing.

Most of all, we're sick of having to stop and explain to people outside the community and its allies as to why we can't just stop and let things be, or wait until it blows over, or wait until times change and we're accepted. None of us are promised that, and if anyone can't understand that, it's hard to move someone so privileged that the status quo doesn't affect them either way in the first place.

Today I sat by a place where 49 members of our community died, and I became more determined than ever to fight against anyone who would see us harmed or worse. Fuck you for doing that, fuck you to anyone who supports it, fuck you to anyone who tries to justify it, fuck you to anyone who makes jokes about it...

And fuck you to anyone who insists on neutrality whenever it's convenient for them, but come out with their hands open when it's safe for their token ally cookie. Our lives are at stake every single day, especially with this fucking xenophobe leading the country, and we don't have time to stop and consider how you might feel about having your shitty word choice corrected, okay Brenda?

Stand with us. Listen to the stories of those you've never been able to understand. Help us prevent something like this ever happening again instead of taking it for granted that it won't. We don't have that luxury.

Ode to the Blocked

You ain't a girl you a man
You aren't a pretty girl
You're fucking ugly
Jesus, keep it to yourself
Why would you ever talk about this
Why would you ever want to do this
Are you sure you don't have multiple personality disorder
Are you sure you're not just depressed
Are you sure you're not just confused
Are you sure you're not just a drag queen
Are you sure you're really Marissa

Why can't you just be gay
Why can't I use the pronouns I know you by
Why can't I call you the name you were born with
Why aren't you just that name
Why aren't you just that body
Why wouldn't you want to keep it
Why wouldn't you want to have more kids
What will the kids say
What will the parents say
What will other people's parents say
What will other people say
How will you ever get a girlfriend acting like this
Don't you want to be a provider
Don't you want to step up and be a man
Don't you want to be a man
Aren't you a man

You're just you to me
You've always just been you

Your gender doesn't matter to me
Your genitals don't matter to me
Nobody cares about your genitals
Gross, do you still have a dick
Are you going to get surgery
Are those tits real
You're so tall
How will you ever pass
Why can't you just do it in private
Why should we have to change
Why should we have to be different
We don't have to accept you

I'm not transphobic but
I just don't want a dick
I just don't consider you a real woman
I'm straight, sorry
You're really cute and everything
But I just like vaginas
You understand right
I'm straight
Not gay
That's all that matters
It would be a dealbreaker
It's confusing
How would I explain to my parents
That I'm dating a tranny

Faggot
Queen
Pillowbiter
Queer
Tranny
Shemale

———

Ladyboy
Dude in a dress
Fake woman
Not a woman
It's just science
It's just biology
It's just Jesus
It's just reality
It's just my opinion, man

You need to calm down
You need to understand other opinions
You're immature
You're lazy
You're pretentious
You're dramatic
You need to lay off the sensitivity hormones
Were you always this much of a bitch
You're just too much for me
You need to stop being so defensive
Not everyone is staring at you
Not everyone is afraid of you
Not everyone wants to hurt you

How will you ever get a girlfriend acting like that
Stop saying no and shut up
Just let me touch you
Fine, stop being such a bitch
Stop resisting
Stop it
Stop it
Take it, bitch
Take it
This is what happens when you play hard to get

This is what happens when you dress the way you do
This is what happens when you are who you are
This is what happens
When you're transgender

You deserve it
You asked for it
You should expect it
What do you expect, look where you are
If you've got a penis, use the men's room
If you're a trans in the men's room, I'll kick your ass
If my masculinity is so fragile, let me hit you
There's no sexism anymore
Feminism isn't necessary
Feminism is outdated
Feminists hate men
Feminists don't need to include transwomen
All women have vaginas
All women were born women
This is how you really feel
This is how you need to act
This is how you need to feel
This is how you need to change
This is how you need to be
To make it easier on me

You give a bad name to transwomen
You're too radical
You're too angry
You're too bold
You're too confrontational
Nothing's ever going to change their mind
Why even bother
Why not just stealth it

Can't you hide your breasts
Who cares what they think
Just ignore it, they'll go away
Just use the family bathroom
What do you expect, it's their opinion
It's how they were raised
It's how they were taught
It's how they were shown religion
It's not something they can identify with

If you cut it off won't it hurt
If you get the surgery, you'll still be a man
You'll still be a man
You'll always be a man
You can't change gender
Gender and sex are the same
Gender and sex can't be changed
I have more of a right to your identity than you do
I know better than you
You're just confused
You're just lost
You're just brainwashed
You're just young and stupid
You're being manipulated by your professors
You're on drugs
You're going to hell
You have no respect for your spouse
How do you think they feel
How do you think I feel
It's going to take time to adjust
Didn't you think about how this would affect me
Are you sure this is right
Are you sure this is you
Are you sure

Hate

From Given Up On to Give it Up

I've told various parts of this story for years, and today is the day that I finally get to conclude this journey. Today is officially my last day as an undergraduate at the University of Pennsylvania, and it took me almost 32 years to get here, and I don't think anyone ever thought I would. Let me explain...

In elementary school, I was bored. First grade saw me reading books while class was going on because I was tired of whatever the teacher was helping the other kids with. Eventually they put me on independent study, because I was reading at a way higher level than the grade would allow, and this continued all the way through fifth grade. It is my belief, in retrospect, that because of this, they weren't looking for anything that would've retrospectively confirmed things like ADHD and gender identity. That, and I was in a snobby, elitist school district that at that time wouldn't have fathomed something like that. Boy how things have changed!

The problem was, by putting me off in a corner and letting me do whatever I wanted for five years, they taught me that I didn't have to pay attention in class, participate, learn how to work in a group, study, take notes, or anything like that. Imagine how that came crashing down once I hit junior high!

Getting into junior high was getting thrown to the wolves, and I never truly recovered. Even in sixth grade, my English teacher put me on the computer separately to write a book to send to President Clinton. Why wouldn't I have assumed this was the way it was always going to be? It was how I was treated. That's why I didn't take to heart any of the warnings from my parents or teachers that I was not living up to my potential. I can't deny my own responsibility in never trying to do so either, but once again, I'd already learned that I could get by and do whatever I wanted because I was really smart. It screwed me over in the long run.

I was also perceived to be a feminine boy, and that got me daily hazing from a variety of bullies. Then I'd go home, and I felt like an outcast from my own family, for reasons I won't get into here. The worst incident was getting beaten with a baseball bat in my own driveway by two boys who called themselves "friends" because I was feminine. Or assumed to be gay.

In high school, the shit hit the fan. I was hospitalized three different times as a result of my ongoing self-crisis, running away from home when things got too much, and my general apathy toward school work. The teachers never forwarded any of the work I missed, so I failed ninth grade. I was emotionally distraught, desperately seeking love and attention, and that I believe covered up any of the aforementioned issues. That, and they'd given up on me. It only took them until tenth grade to do that.

They gave me a choice: reform school, or going to Florida to live with my grandmother so I could take the GED. I was an emotionally charged kid, but I wasn't a criminal. I never got in any real trouble. The only time I was ever in the back of a police car was when they found me after I'd run away. I didn't drink or do drugs, I was just desperate for love. And misdiagnosed with BPD.

In Florida, you can get your GED at age 16, as opposed to Pennsylvania, where your class has to graduate first. I aced the first test, so they didn't think I needed the classes. But then they said I needed a second test, and I aced that too. Then, that's where my grandmother says I really messed up, because at the actual GED test, I got one question wrong. Ruined everything! I got a real high school diploma instead of a GED because of that, so technically I graduated high school with a 4.0, despite passing exactly zero years.

It was around that time that I was in a small play at Little Theater. I was talking about my plans to get an early start at HACC and get ahead of the game, and there was this guy. Let's call him Will C. He said, and I quote: "Yeah, you go ahead and go to HACC. Then one day you'll be working for me." I don't know why that of all things stuck in my craw to this day, but it did. I hated him so much for it, because he'd always been cruel to me, snide, making remarks, and generally being a dick in my direction. I never forgot it.

I tried that whole HACC thing, but all of those problems were still problems. That, and being 17 years old, pretending to be male, and suddenly surrounded by gorgeous college women, I was going insane. I bombed out, and did pretty much the same thing at age 20 when I tried again.

I spent years working in retail, until I landed a pretty good gig working at Nordstrom at Mall of America. The average take-home was more than I'd ever seen in my life. One problem: they never bothered to tell me that it was seasonal. I moved halfway across the country for a seasonal job, and I was stuck yet again.

I moved home in August, and that weekend, the girlfriend who'd stuck with me the whole time cheated on me. So I was jobless, single, and seemingly without any path whatsoever. I went to my mother, who works at HACC, and said: "get me back into school, I don't care what it takes. I'm never going to let this happen to me again."

I got back into HACC. They let me only take two classes, and one of them was English Composition. I remember after the second class, the professor pulled me aside afterward and said, "what are you doing here?" It was my Billy Joel "Piano Man" moment. Despite the issues focusing, sitting still, and trying to cope with what I'd eventually understand to be my gender identity, I was destroying it.

I spent two years at HACC, and only got one B. The rest were A's. This got me into Phi Theta Kappa, the honor's society for community colleges. I was writing for the school paper, being published, and getting offers from all over the country. But once again, I had a girl in my life, and wanting to stay with her, I was looking for an option that would allow me to stay with her and pursue higher academia. That's when Penn (not Penn State) had a session at HACC. I thought to myself, "wow, I could take the Amtrak everyday and come home to her! This will be great!"

Penn was the only place I applied. Penn was the only place I was accepted. Fall 2013, I started at Penn. They gave me the impression that it would take two years to graduate, but then they only took six of my classes as transfers, and only one was used as anything but a free elective. I essentially went to college for two years to get into college.

The first two years, I commuted via Amtrak, and it averaged being late or canceled about half the time. Plus, there were two trains leaving back to Harrisburg: 8:15 and 11pm. Having to take night classes (damn LPS), most of the classes ended at 8 or 8:30. So I could either leave class early, which they didn't care for, or find three hours to kill, usually at a bar, get home around 1am, and do the whole thing over. Halfway through, I started driving instead, and that unleashed a whole new set of problems: I-76, the Sure-Kill. It doesn't matter what time of day you hit that road, you will inevitably be in stopped traffic.

The girlfriend I had broke up with me at the end of the first semester. I still continued this commute, because I was determined to see it through. That, and I met my would-be husband soon after. I was dealing with all these feelings that were finally bubbling to the surface as well. Was I a girl? Had I been a girl this whole time? What was this going to mean? Would anyone ever accept me? Could I be safe in this world?

Then I won the 2015 Hershey Student Film Festival with a film I wrote about suicide, something near and dear to me, and a huge problem at Penn. That was the last film I'd ever write though, because as I learned, I have a degree in cinema to learn that I don't really like cinema all that much. But I still dealt with the internal struggle of gender identity, which was delayed for almost two years by people who didn't bother to learn about consent.

You all know the Pastor Carl story. That was how I kicked down the closet door and became who I truly am. Within months, I was out to the school and the world, had my name legally changed, affirmed my identity, been on HRT, and published two books during that time. The podcast grew into a huge success, I met so many new friends, guested on dozens more podcasts, and saw bookings for speeches, lectures, and appearances start to roll in. School became secondary, and after four years of a 100-mile daily each way commute four times a week, I was not only out of gas, but different opportunities and activities were taking my attention. I was no longer the 27-year-old pretend male with hopes and aspirations of a 4.0. I was a married 31-year-old transwoman finding success on her own and running her own business. As I used the metaphor many times, I had to take a knee and run out the clock, because I had no more energy to give to Penn academics. I needed to get through the last semester passing, and that's all I cared.

Finally, my issues with language were taken care of after a year-plus of trying. I accepted neurodivergence, was exempted from having to learn a foreign language, and that saved my college career. It's literally that I cannot do it, I can't process it, and without that exemption, I was never going to graduate. It took getting a second evaluation and pressing hard to do so, but it finally happened. That, and CAPS doctors helped me get the medical assistance I needed with ADHD, anxiety, and the one that truly surprised me, PTSD. That explained my night terror attacks, my over-sensitivity to bright lights, loud sounds, and being startled. Dealing with all of this, the gender transition, the commute, not to mention an Ivy League education despite never having passed a year of high school and having to work through it, definitely took its toll on everything. I'm amazed I can still wake up in the morning.

But this morning I did. I finally reached it. The last day of undergrad. Six years of college, plus years of being confused, tortured, bullied, misunderstood, and doubted have finally culminated in this. So, I can only say one thing on this momentous day of finally completing a journey...

Fuck you, Will C.

And thank you. I couldn't have done it without you.

2014

If you know anything about me, you know why the year of 2014 is significant.

That was the year I first started to come out.

That was the first time in my life I felt the sense of overwhelming joy that I'm now awash in.

That was the first time that my naive nature got me in trouble.

That was the first time I truly understood what is the queer reality.

Or, as some people might say it, shit we made up for attention.

Let me explain...

In 2014, I was introduced to terms that more accurately described what I was. For so long, I was in the assumption that I was a drag queen and nothing more, because I didn't know there was an option beyond that. Once I started learning, the floodgates of so many years of hiding opened up.

The problem is, I wasn't socialized as a woman. I wasn't taught things that women have to watch out for. I didn't know things like "be careful in a dark alley" or "don't accept a drink unseen" or "be careful who you're drunk around." These thoughts never would've occurred to me, and there's something seriously fucked up about that. Both that they happened, and that they had to.

I'm sick of people marginalizing the experience of trauma victims, and I'm sick of people always having to play the Devil's Advocate when someone explains their experience, their trauma, or their identity. They're always looking for the benefit of the doubt so that they don't have to take any action on their part whatsoever. That would require changing thinking and we can't have that.

There's the terrible myth that anyone AMAB can't be raped, whether it's because of physical reaction or because they always want it. There's the myth that we're somehow asking for it, or that we deserve it for being freaks. There's people who think it didn't happen, or think we're exaggerating, or who are always looking to find a reason why they either can one-up or disregard what you're saying.

When I was roofied, another transwoman told me that I probably just couldn't handle my liquor, because "it seems strange that someone would use roofies on you and not bother to go ahead and rape you."

Of all people, shouldn't we who've been through that experience know better? Can't we be better than that without victim-blaming and marginalizing someone who has been through trauma?
I came out again in 2016, but that was after almost two years of complete misery. Hiding, denial, numbness, blaming myself, and everything in between: what would my family think, would I lose my kids, would I lose my job, would I ever be okay?

Then I was. Sort of.

Everyone who has only known me for the last few months, they see the ridiculous schedule and output I have, but they don't always know what came before it. The disasters I suffered and the numbness, tears, self-doubt, self-hating, and the denial destroyed me inside before I finally started to accept who I was, and it clicked all at once in the face of a hate pastor.

But that took two years. Two years of denying I was Marissa. Two years of pretending to be male. Two years of pretending to be straight. Two years of my life lost because someone thought my consent was theirs for the taking. Twice.

Then some people are quick to jump on the "faking it" claim. Once again, because that's easier than actually doing something about it.

The Power of the Medium

The rise of Nazi power in the 1930s saw the use and application of the recent technological innovation of film among its many tactics in assuming control over the country. It is without a doubt that the most infamous example of the cinematic advocation of this very process was captured by Leni Riefenstahl's *Triumph of the Will* (1933), a documentary displaying Adolf Hitler's speeches in Nuremberg. While Riefenstahl herself later claimed that she was filming a documentary and not conveying any political message with them, if we are to assume a McLuhan perspective on the film, then it is without a doubt that Riefenstahl's inventive and specific techniques set a political narrative that contributed to the rise of Nazi power through the regime leader Adolf Hitler.

Any film theorist, as well as any expert on communication or language, will emphasize the importance of non-verbal communication, or in layman's terms, what's not being said says an awful lot. Riefenstahl's films are no exception. It's not enough to have captured Adolf Hitler's speeches to Nuremberg, something that alone probably could not be misconstrued as objective in and of itself, but it's the methods and techniques that were used in the process that definitively communicate otherwise.

Susan Sontag describes *Triumph of the Will* as "the most successfully, most purely propagandistic film ever made, whose very conception negates the possibility of the film maker's having an aesthetic or visual conception independent of propaganda. (Sontag, 1975)" While her (refuted) resistance to Goebbels trying to dictate the visual representation of the film may show that she wasn't a drone completely following orders, it would be irresponsible to suggest that her visuals aren't aware of these techniques that made propaganda films so successful. Nazi Germany's use of propaganda shows heavy influence from the era of Soviet Montage, despite Goebbels' best effort to distance themselves from the Bolsheviks.

Riefenstahl was given resources directly from the German government, and allowed the budget that enabled the creation of dozens of cinematic inventions that are still used today. To see them objectively and deny their influence is irresponsible, as difficult as it is to associate with someone capturing the image of Adolf Hitler in such a light. "She [Riefenstahl] had an unlimited budget, a crew of 120, and a huge number of cameras. (Sontag 1975)" The entire Nuremberg rally was created with the idea of making it a film in mind. Otherwise, the low angle shots from the front of Hitler's podiums would've been impossible. A rut had to be dug in front of the stage to provide the space for the camera and its movements from such angles, and without the cooperation of the Nazi government in planning and aiding Riefenstahl's efforts, they likely would've been for naught. Sometimes the lack of interference is as powerful as visible influence. "She was able to set up special camera positions, which included a camera lift on an iron flag mast in the stadium," Alan Sennett details. "There was also to be an opportunity to restage shots at a later date. (Sennett, 2014)"

As with the influence of an unlimited budget and a lack of interference, not everything in regard to the visual medium is direct and blatant. The Soviets throughout the 1920s made use of the "Cinema Eye" and advocated for the training of direct responses to the human body. Or, put another way, certain imagery and information could draw programmed behavior and thought patterns that were instinctive as opposed to learned. Riefenstahl's films uses several of these as well, especially in the form of generating the unspoken comparative and contrasting natures of the figures in the film. "Many devices are employed for the sole purpose of eliciting from audience certain specific responses," explains Siegfried Kracauer in *From Caligari to Hitler*. "In this film, marching infantry columns betoken an advance; in it, the ideal type of German soldier emerges time and again in close-up, a soft face that involuntarily betrays the close relationship of soul and blood, sentimentality, and sadism. (Kracauer, 2004)"

Perhaps another, more notorious example, sees Hitler flying into Nuremberg itself. To the modern eyes of a viewer, this would not strike the mind as unusual, but both cinema and flight were new innovations in the early 1930s. The very idea of filming a landing plane was unheard of, and the image of Hitler descending from the clouds allowed him to assume a godlike status over the rest of his citizens. "National Socialism would, of course, have been unthinkable without all the genres, movements, and images from which it borrowed," explains Linda Shulte-Sasse. "It builds on a foundation of modernism and uses nostalgia to 'colonize the fantasy life' (Rentschler) of its constituency. (Schulte-Sasse, 1991)" The blend of new technology and nostalgic appeal for the homeland come together in these brilliantly-captured visual technological feats, and thus were so effective for, among other reasons, Riefenstahl's application and comprehension of the power of framing. To show Hitler is one thing; but to frame him as a god on Earth could not have been conveyed by accident.

This power, and the visibility reinforcing such, did not only involve the placement of Adolf Hitler. Kracauer's central point in *From Caligari to Hitler* argues for the idea of the "mass ornament," in which a group of people move as one, like a machine. The military demonstrations taking place before Hitler show not only complete and unquestioned solidarity, but from the high-perched perspective of Hitler, he looks down upon them from great height, as he would have when descending from the clouds into Nuremberg earlier in the film. "There is a constant panning, traveling, tilting up and down - so that the spectators not only see passing a feverish world, but feel themselves uprooted in it," Kracauer elaborates. "Mass ornaments appeared to Hitler and his staff, who must have appreciated them as configurations and symbolizing the readiness of the masses to be shaped and used at will by their leaders. (Kracauer, 2004)"

Loyalty can be shown in the movement of a group of people unified as one, like the machine-like qualities theorized by Soviet Montage filmmakers a decade earlier. The mass ornament takes this idea one step further. Not only are the natural and subconscious reactions captured and co-opted with a specific purpose in mind, the idea of unity with the Führer for home and country is transposed with emotional appeal and manipulation. This could not be anything but intentional on the part of Leni Riefenstahl.

Consider also the power of the symbol: Not only is the swastika unmistakably tied to Nazi power, but Hitler himself as well. In *Triumph of the Will*, the swastikas and the huge flags displaying them prominently were featured in nearly every shot. In the same way that symbolism can be used to convey a message, the symbol itself being so prominent associates itself with the person being featured. In this case, Adolf Hitler and the swastika become bound with Germany, victory, success, and the cause. To elaborate further, the actions that transpire around the Führer, in addition to the mass ornament sequences and placement of the gaze of Hitler, other space in the film is filled with traditional German values meant to restore a feeling of calmness, nostalgia, and aspiration. Women are shown as homemakers and mothers of the children. Little boys play at war, for they one day too will lead Germany to great success and carry on its power for generations. While this reinforcement can be jarring to modern eyes in some capacity, at the time it showed a unified, traditional German population in complete collusion with its leader, the symbol of its leader, and the army that served under them.

Taking into account the previous decade of uncertainty and economic strife in Germany, the transformative nature of seeing someone appearing to have Germany's best interests at heart was even more powerful, considering the circumstances. This created a reality in Germany that had been long suffering in depression and uncertainty from the crushing loss of the first World War. A rise to power again for Germany not only meant the change in guard would bring about the end of the suffering, but the rise of those who cooperated with the one taking place with Adolf Hitler himself: One country, one people, one leader. The individual no longer mattered. "In such scenes, the Nazi rulers' contempt for the individual becomes apparent. (Kracauer, 2004)" An individual can think independently, perhaps against the will of the improvement and success of the Fatherland, and is therefore abhorred against the image of the mass ornament showing the unity of Germany under Adolf Hitler. The Führer is the only individual, a father and a god to all of his citizens, rescuing them from the depths of despair and making Germany great again (comparison intentional) can only function with the questioning and criticism of its leader rendered equivalent with treason and an anti-German sentiment.

To control the media is to control reality itself. "This film represents an inextricable mixture of a show simulating German reality and of German reality maneuvered into a show. (Kracauer, 2004)" When reality becomes a show, there's a disconnect between that reality and the negative effects, such as suffering, depression, violence, and death. A god cannot die; therefore, Germany will not die under the rule of Adolf Hitler. Creating that cognitive dissonance within its citizens eliminates the fear of death in multiple ways. First, under the protection of a god, many religions teach that one will live forever. The savior of Germany being Adolf Hitler, he has pulled Germany from the depths from which they escaped, never to return. Second, an economic depression the likes of which Germany suffered was inescapably stricken and connected with death, so to rise like the phoenix from the ashes, Germany does not die again with Hitler, but continues to rise and live on, as the suffering has ended and now, the true potential and greatness of Germany can be unlocked under the guidance and love of its father, its god, its Führer.

To blend what is a show with reality does not create the ability of a citizenry to discern the difference. When the entire media is controlled and specifically designed against individualism and questioning of the government, and the government controls the media, what the government says is reality. Riefenstahl visually connects these ideas with the thread of presentation and visual establishment throughout. Germany becomes the blend of the modern power and nostalgic morality to create its own contemporary reality. "...All construct aestheticized images of Germany's cultural to create a sense of collective identity in the present, to inspire the spectator to celebrate the consciousness of being 'German' - a consciousness that can be carried beyond the theater. (Schulte-Sasse, 1991)" Controlling history through the present and consolidating the two creates a uniform reality specifically dictated and presented by the government for its citizens, in which all the information is communicated with the intention of subjugating its citizens under the guise of a united Germany.

These are the very foundations of propaganda. Riefenstahl's denied connections to abetting the communication of such propaganda seems foolish when contrasted with the product that exists. "Arguments that appeal to something an audience perceives to be true or real may permit the propagandist to gain its trust," describes Alan Sennett. "Yet the appeal to 'truth' in propaganda is not an end in itself but rather a means to an end. It appears to validate the claim of the propagandist to be revealing of life as it actually is. (Sennett, 2014)" What is real does not matter as much as what is believed to be real. Connecting the two allows a dictation of reality to become reality, and appealing to the audience's emotions and need for comfort, salvation, and solidarity becomes an effective medium through which to unify a previously-shattered nation. After all, if the only alternative is to return to the days of a broken country with no identity, how could a single collective identity with a prominently-displayed symbol and a voice of this identity not be persuasive?

Editing is also a choice that inescapably creates subjectivity, and *Triumph* is no exception. To show one thing and not another is a subjective choice made by the creator of the film, and the two hours of film for *Triumph* were cut down from a great deal more than that, which demonstrates the fact that specific choices were made to communicate a narrative. To take hours upon hours of film and condense it into a consumable package with a driving story and intent prominently featured, it need not be truly objective, but only have the appearance of being so. Or, as Alan Sennett further explains, "Documentaries cannot be deemed to portray 'reality' simply because the camera becomes the spectator. The viewer's gaze is directed at whatever the filmmaker desires him or her to see. While the subject matter is real enough, the image is a construction and perhaps a distortion of reality. (Sennett, 2014)" It doesn't have to be real; it only has to feel real to the viewer. Nothing else matters at that point.

To summarize, Leni Riefenstahl claimed objectivity in the name of only filming a documentary as a reason that she did not have any political message behind her film *Triumph of the Will*. However, the evidence in the film suggests selective editing, carefully planned camera shots, the implementation of the mass ornament, and the specific positioning of Hitler in relation to the masses and soldiers. Therefore, it can be reasonably concluded that Riefenstahl's film had a deliberate, intentional message to go along with the illusion of reality it created of Hitler's Germany. Any other claims to objectivity become extremely difficult to measure when weighted against the overwhelming evidence, film theory, history, and sequence of events that transpired over those days in Nuremberg, and the effect the film had on its citizens is equally undeniable.

Works Cited

Kracauer, Siegfried, and Leonardo Quaresima. *From Caligari to Hitler: A Psychological History of the German Film.* , 2004.

Schulte-Sasse, Linda. "Leni Riefenstahl's Feature Films and the Question of a Fascist Aesthetic." *Cultural Critique*, no. 18, 1991, pp. 123–148.

Sennett, Alan. "Film Propaganda: Triumph of the Will as a Case Study." *Framework: The Journal of Cinema and Media* 55.1 (2014): 45-65.

Sontag, Susan. "Fascinating Fascism." *Under the Sign of Saturn.* New York, N.Y.: Farrar, Strauss, and Giroux, 1980. 73-105. Rpt. in *Contemporary Literary Criticism,* Ed. Tom Burns and Jeffrey W. Hunter. Vol. 190. Detroit: Gale, 2004. *Literature Resource Center.*

I'm Not Confused

You're just confused, they'd say
Going to grow up one day
And everything will be just fine
You have a history like mine
And it's going to be okay
These feelings will remain
But one day they'll change
You'll be better for it
If only you can ignore it
And avoid the extra pain
You can't be a girl
You were born in this world
As a man, you should be
Proud to be a he
Go ahead, give it a whirl
You'll know when the time
When you reach your prime
That everything will make sense
If you let go of the pretense
That you have in your mind
You shouldn't be feminine
Your genetics are masculine
And you're going to stick out
If you choose to pick out
Against society's judgment
You'll never be right
You'll be out of sight
From what makes us great
Or the potential for a date
You'll be lonely on Saturday night
Put away the eyeliner
It's not even for guyliner
Nobody wants you in mascara

You're likely to scare a
Mother, sister, or someone finer
Than your wildest dreams
Better than it seems
Could be the one you need
To make your life proceed
You'll know what it means
Look at your birth certificate
You'll never get a duplicate
That changes your gender mark
You've got the wrong part
And you'll never change it
Be happy with who you are
Get a job and a car
And a wife and have kids
And at life you'll win
Before you even start
That's what they told me
That's me who they see
But they don't understand
That I can't be a man
I'm not meant to be
The one who takes charge
The one who stands large
Is always the big spoon
Punches out the goon
And leaves Biff on his car
This is who I am inside
I hold tremendous pride
Of living as I truly am
Doing the best I can
Even those nights I cried
You can't take it from me
My masculinity

Wasn't something to question
Or mock for your own fun
Because I wanted to be pretty
Of the girls, I'm one
Disagree and you're done
Being a part of my social life
Goddammit, I'm the wife
And spiro leaves me with none
So take your T level
And your imaginary devil
And leave me the fuck alone
I don't care if you condone
This, I'm not a social rebel
I've been a girl this whole time
I wasted my years of prime
Living up to your expectation
Pretending my relation
To girls was on the line
Only as a precaution
For the day they might shun
Me for who I really was
And they'd do it because
Being trans isn't masculine
What about the children
What do you think will happen
When they find out about you
They'll soon be without you
Because of you living in sin
But only the children know
Where these arguments will go
They don't have your knack
Or instinct to attack
Anyone who might be different, so
Don't shield them or excuse

Your shitty opinion from the news
That from us they need protection
As if the birth gender defection
Means we're on a bathroom cruise
Inside that closed stall
Don't you want it all
Every time you've gone in there
Do you search for a pair
Do you stand outside and call
Do you have a dick
Is this some kind of trick
I might have to assault you
If you're one of those who
Was born with a prick
Or I'll try to screw you
But that's only if you
Keep it on the down low
I don't want to let them know
Dating trannies is so taboo
You gotta keep it a secret
And only reveal it
When I'm in the mood
To be exotic and rude
What an amazing existence
I'm not for your fantasy
I'm not here to be
A fetish object to ogle
I'm living to struggle
For those who matter to me
I'll yell and scream
And fight and dream
Until we no longer have to
And when a guy coming at you
Won't be something threatening

I'll just pass by
No longer having to lie
About my real identity
Who I'm supposed to be
Who would know better than I
I'm Marissa McCool
Don't be a fucking fool
And don't ask what's under my dress
Or you'll end up a mess
I'll make you look like a tool
I am who I am
I don't have to demand
My right to exist
So if there's anything I missed
Remember I'm not a man
I'm a girl, I'm a she
I rejoice in femininity
And I have no reason to doubt
So look at me again, inside and out
And learn my true identity

Snapshot of Transcience

To be free
To live true
To let go of the burden of secret
Is to truly see the world.

The blade of a pine,
A snow-covered mountain,
The everbrightening shimmer
Of the morning sun
Over quickly melting snow;

I see the colors anew,
The nature therapy
Checks me in
As a returning guest.

All around me
The sentiment of serenity
The spectacle of unconquered,
I am rendered
As a mere humbled patron
Of its healing grace.

Departing is so sorrow,
Walking over again
The tracks created
To reach the momentary
Blissful seconds of clarity.

But a selected glimpse
Though it may be
Toward the mountains
Yet to climb

Along the seemingly infinite horizon,
My journey is no longer
Perpetually weighed down
By the heaviest of unseen burdens:
The burdening secret
Of identity.

I am far more
Than a sum
Of the parts I didn't choose.

I am the Planet of one,
The waking oblivion of bliss,
The anxious headspace
Of the purple girl Ris.

Though a long way
To go remains,
I travel lighter
Having shed the baggage
With the mask of my former shield.

I walk the more dangerous path
By choice of not to hide,
But they who've embraced me
Shelter me from
Any pangs of regret
For which I may search
Among the discarded.

This is true,
This is right,
This is me,
The me that you knew,

But the mirror did not
Until I gazed
At the correct reflection.

Previously untouched,
Formerly shamed,
Now a cloud of the spirit
Of mystic joy;
I am now but a protected
Nomad of these parts,
And I'm for long so grateful
Of permission of minute occupation
Along the intersecting trails
Of your own journeys
Yet untraveled.

I Don't Have to Think You're a Bad Person To Find Your Opinions Shitty

There isn't one second of the day that I'm not grateful for what has happened in my life, the last few months especially. I'm now legally myself, and I have the correct gender marker on my driver's license. The projects I've pursued have gained me the pleasure of knowing many new people, and I am not for one second ignorant of that.

However, I can't say it's been a path of no resistance.

When you write a book that starts by saying "fuck you," it's going to have some backlash. It comes with the territory, and I'm not denying that. But sometimes when you get misinterpreted, it gets frustrating. When you get corrected by someone, it depends on the correction, and the person giving it. But when things are assumed about you, you're told you're downright wrong, or you're instructed on how to do your own job, that's when I start getting annoyed.

There are those who tell me that I don't understand the mind or mentality of certain people, and they're absolutely right. For instance, the biggest reason I've loathed country music all my life is that the people who listened to that music when I was growing up beat the shit out of me pretty regularly. I'd hear these songs about beer, girls in blue jeans, pickup trucks, and campfires, and I'd associate them with pain, isolation, and anguish. Then I was expected to embrace that very subculture, even want to be a part of it, but it could never happen. Not with my experience, regardless of my identity.

Notice that I didn't say I didn't like country music fans there. That's personal. I don't care for a certain subculture. That's not the same thing as disrespecting the people within it.

The same goes for Donald Trump voters.

Now, let me be clear: the ones driving the anti-trans bus, the ones trying to push us back in the closet, the ones trying to force their religion on everyone else, and the ones trying to legislate discrimination as long as it's their beliefs oppressing everyone else's can all go fuck themselves. That's not what I'm talking about. Let's just say that I've had to converse with some Trump supporters who want to tell me that they're not all like that, and they're right. I never said they were, nor do I think anyone who votes a certain way is a bad person, necessarily.

But understand that I don't have the luxury of that levity. Our community does not have that luxury. And there's nothing more insulting than someone from without; for instance, a straight cis white man; telling me that my perspective of the world is wrong.

The same way that I don't understand the perspective of a Donald Trump voter or a country music fan, I also don't technically know the perspective of a straight cis white man. I passed as one for a long time, but it was all a mask; a mask that I threw off once I couldn't take it anymore.

But that doesn't mean I have to respect your opinion either.

I do not know what it's like to be you. I cannot possibly fathom how you can look at this bumbling, arrogant, thin-skinned, disrespectful person and think: "yeah, that's how a person should act, let alone the leader of the free world." Most of the time when that discussion is had, deferments are made instead of actual arguments: but her emails, but Obama, but Pennywise...

Changing the subject is not an argument. Irrelevant comparison is not an argument.

And neither is telling a queer person what the world is actually like.

Once again, I point out the fact that I don't understand the perspective of a Trump voter. I can have that dissonance. But how in the everloving holy fuck is a straight cis person going to explain the queer experience to me? They've tried, to the point of telling me that I'm wrong, dumb, incorrect, warped, stupid, crazy, ignorant, and beyond. Or worse, I'm told that no one actually has a problem with queer people and that I'm bitching and whining about nothing.

Fuck you.

I acknowledge that I'm a privileged queer person. I have an audience, a platform, and a university and family that supports and acknowledges my identity. But to say that my perspective of what it's like in the world being visibly queer is wrong, especially coming from someone who could not be less that? No. Sorry.

There is a political party in this country that has done all they can to fuck with us. It won them a goddamn election in 2004, because gay people getting the right to marry would do something to the social fabric or whatever. Two years ago, an argument over who can use the fucking bathroom put us on a hypervigilant that has not subsided since. I've had to ask people to walk to the bathroom with me. I've had to ask people to walk me to my car. I've been sexually assaulted. I've been threatened. I've been misgendered. I've been disrespected. And to suggest that none of these things are issues is to deny that I understand my own experience of the world.

No more that I can tell a straight cis person what it's like to be who they are, nobody who has not lived with that experience can tell me that I'm wrong about it. Sure, queer acceptance is at an all-time high. However, there's now a bus traveling the country openly dehumanizing us. Milo Fuckface targets people and says they're mentally ill, and the only time people develop a problem with him is when he makes favorable remarks about a child molester. Politicians treat us like an inhuman sexual predator drone, which inevitably has people patrolling the bathrooms looking to fuck with some transpeople, and makes us super self conscious and paranoid.

Why, you might ask? Because you never know who you're going to walk by when you're openly queer. You never know who is going to rage that you're holding hands with someone of the same gender. You never know who is going to decide to murder you for being trans, and though I cannot speak personally to this part of the experience, especially if you're a person of color. Eight this year have been murdered already for having the nerve to exist.

We do not make the choice to be who we are. Our choices lie in how open we choose to be about it. We are often reduced to "what goes on in the bedroom" or "the privacy of your own home" but that is bullshit. No straight or cis person is told that they can only be who they are in private, and nobody ever should. That's fucking bullshit for anyone to say to anyone. We are not a sum of our parts, and we are not only queer for what we do in the bedroom. That reduces us to sexual acts, which is what our detractors think of us as anyway, and the whole vicious circle begins again. But some people want to tell me these things don't exist?

You don't know the half of it. Even if every single person you knew didn't mind queer people and never committed a single hateful act toward one, it's still anecdotal. Unless you're following me around, cataloguing every interaction I have, and documenting the non-verbal ones, there's no way you could possibly know my experience, and I wouldn't expect you to. But to dismiss all of what I say based on not agreeing with it is to accuse me of false representation of myself, of making things up, of creating a situation to supposedly whine about when there are real life and death issues facing our community every day. But it makes you uncomfortable when I talk about that, and that means I'm supposed to talk about something else? Not gonna happen.

You still elected a person who has advocated for doing so. Even if that's not the reason you voted for him, you voted for him despite it, and your choice put all of us in danger. But I'm supposed to give everyone a pass because... You don't like it, I guess? Nope, sorry.

That's why I speak up. That is why I'm open about my experiences. Because so many queer and transpeople either cannot, will not, or aren't in a position where they can. I know I'm lucky for what I have, but don't for a second think that means I'm free of danger. I risk violence and worse simply by existing, but being loud and critical while being queer is doubling down on that. It's a situation you cannot possibly empathize with, and not being able to doesn't make you a bad person. Your shitty opinion that you think you know who I am better than I do, though? Yeah, I'm going to call that out.

Most of the time, I think these comments have good intentions. I don't think most people set out to be shitty to another person. But perhaps when a minority speaks up, you might want to listen to what they have to say before you dismiss it or defend yourself. The fact that you're even talking to us probably means that we're not talking about you anyway. Good intentions don't mean that the results aren't shitty though. While someone may be trying to get me to see a different perspective, assuming or correcting my perspective and experience only comes across as condescending and disrespectful. It'd be like me trying to tell a trans person of color what their experience is. Sure, I have certain similarities, but I've never lived that existence, and it would be foolish of me to think I know better than they do. That is the only reason I don't speak up about that more than I do; I cannot speak to that experience, except to say that the targeting of transpeople of color is sickening, and something needs to be done about it.

One last thing... There's a particular comment recently that had something that stuck in my craw beyond what I've discussed here, as these are generalized criticisms I've received since coming out, not referencing any in particular. The funny thing is, this one had nothing to do with my experience, but simply a complete lack of regard for who I am. If you're reading this, you're probably already pissed at me, but allow me to say the following first, and yes, this applies to everyone:

1. Don't EVER tell me what to write, especially on my blog. I decide what I write about.

2. Don't EVER talk about my genitals. Especially bringing them up in a post that didn't even mention

them. Unless you're my husband or girlfriend, it's none of your fucking business.

3. You can call me many things... Some true, some less so... But to say that I have no tangible skills and a lazy work ethic? That goes beyond being wrong... It's downright offensive. I can't tell you how many people have seen that comment and laughed their asses off, because it takes knowing very little of who I am to say something so profoundly incorrect.

First, I've been in the work force for 17 years. I have management experience, have a list pages long of professional references, and worked through college as well. It's easy to assume that all I do is write and podcast, but that is to be ignorant of anything beyond my creative projects, as if I sit and write about wrestling or social justice all day, and then do absolutely nothing else.

Second, a lazy work ethic may be the dumbest thing anyone has ever said about me, ever. It doesn't take knowing much about me to know that the amount of time and care I put into my projects alone speaks to the notion otherwise. I created, host, edit, publish, and promote my own podcast, and I co-host on two others. I just started my eighth book, and third since November. I write two columns a week, maintain a blog, release one podcast a week consistently and on time, appear regularly as a guest on other podcasts, have a photography business, travel to work with other people, and all of this is under the umbrella of my own business which I started with the help of a Harvard lawyer who is also my business manager and laughed harder than anyone at the notion that I might be lazy.

Beyond creative projects, I've been commuting 100 miles each way four days a week to an Ivy League school, and that was after two years of community college, so essentially I've been a full-time college student for six years. It's only been this long because almost nothing transferred, so I had to do it over again. So I did all those aforementioned creative projects WHILE maintaining my education at an elite level under those circumstances with that daily commute while working the entire time, being a wife, being a girlfriend, being a parent, being a friend, and traveling all over the country on top of it. I've worked in over five states THIS FUCKING MONTH! I'm writing this from goddamned Vermont! In five weeks I will graduate one of the top ten universities in this country under these circumstances after not having passed a year of high school when I was younger, and then working for a decade to get enough stability to manage something like this.

I have worked my ass off for more than half my life, most of it with no cushion or safety net, and I'll be damned if someone who doesn't even know me calls me lazy. I'm more than happy to discuss the other things, and my issues with those opinions are made quite clear in this piece, but don't EVER fucking call me lazy again. I've had people ask me to write books on both my work ethic and my time management. Again, I don't think you're a bad person, but I am going to disrespect the fuck out of that opinion, because it's a shitty fucking opinion and deserves to be pointed out as such.

I've strived for kindness in any critical response I've gotten, and I will continue to do my best until I am disrespected. But don't ever presume to tell me my experience is wrong, especially when you couldn't ever possibly begin to empathize with it, and know who the fuck you're talking about when you use words to describe a person in a critical manner. My work ethic was lazy as far as you could tell? Well, you weren't looking very hard then, and I'd suggest reaching out to the person before posting such things in public where they're not likely to be met with the most positive of responses. I am more than willing to engage anyone in conversation about differing opinions, but challenging my work ethic isn't an opinion. It's ignorance, and I'd appreciate it if you and anyone else who criticizes me would recognize that from now on.

And if you like my writing about wrestling but not what I say about other issues, I'd suggest sticking with the wrestling writing, where the most controversial thing I say is that Randy Orton segments of television make me yearn for something more exciting, like Roman Reigns reciting the unabridged dictionary after taking downers.

I am Marissa Alexa McCool. I fought like hell for that name, and I've been through hell to get it. I do the best I can to accommodate all perspectives, opinions, and insights, but I will not tolerate someone telling me that my own story is wrong. Not a chance in hell.

A Hope for Marais

The cyan guide along the mighty lake
Disappears into the gathering of vapor
That fancies itself water mountains.
No skyline of steel could match
The vigor of such geological imitation
Gathering upon our distant horizon.
The harbor of regression fills out
The dark matter of the in-between;
Our sanctuary of frozen crests
Sculpts itself among the few sources
Of ambiance along the pebbled pathway.
My arms spread wide and flicker through
The pure yet frozen invisible exhale
From the infinite waves of indigo bliss.
Skipping into the interactive photograph
The capturing of which many only dream,
I'm allowed to spread my wings
And disconnect from all the social gravities.
My own planet intersects its orbit
Not only with the scenery of our magnificence,
But our own force of triumphant defiance
Over those who would wish us foul.
You permit my decorated drifting,
Seeing me dance along the crooked stones
On which my giddy leaps are provided
Resistance otherwise ending in ice baths,
But you letting me fly my own course
Draws me back to you with greater returns,
Among them being your glittering smile
And the warming comfort of your embrace.
Here, I am free. I spread my wings
And soar with the gulls and loons,

But reaching back down, grasping your hand,
And bringing you with me
For my brief capturing of pure sentiment
Is of no volition but my own.

Silent Dreams

When I dream of what you did to me, I do not have a face. I do not see it through my own eyes. I do not remember what it was like to be there.

I am instead caught in a dream; a moment where you took from me something I can never get back, where you delayed the process of me finally shedding years of burden and hiding. You took that from me.

And yet it feels like a dream; a moment caught in time and memory that transcends reality and stands still in the depths of my past where there is no sound. Nothing. Not a moment of what you may have said, did, or heard, but a soundtrack of nothingness.

You exist there. You have a name, a story, a personality, but your words were not heard, the same as you were unable to hear mine, or at least the only one that mattered: No.

No. I didn't want it. But that didn't matter. You took that from me, and thus my dreams are silenced like the cry of a vampire upon the sun rising. I become nothingness, and my face is vacant.

These silent dreams occur every night, so in one small way, though it be notorious, you will live forever, etched in the stone of the caverns of my heart. You achieved immortality by breaking my consent, and now you will remain there for future anthropologists to find an interpret.

I hope in the depths of time, justice will find you. For no authority exists yet in this world or the next that can interpret the dreams of silence. But I anticipate when they can, for maybe I can once again see myself in my own dream.

ONCE UNSPOKEN - A Monologue

To the world, I'm 31. To myself, I'm 13.
13 years ago, that's when I got my name.
The name that would stick in my mind,
The name I would crave to be called,
The name that made me cry at night,
The name that made me wish it'd gone away,
That was the name that stayed in my heart.

A drag queen is what I thought I was,
Because I didn't know any better.
We weren't educated on such things.
Even the open-minded among us,
To our groups, conversations, and movies,
Transpeople existed only as
Jokes
Punch-Lines
Comedy
Fodder
Plot Twists.
That was all we knew.

Drag queen is what I let them call me,
To pretend that I was laughing with them,
Instead of believing the laughter was at me.
But I loved the makeup, the clothes, the shoes,
The way my eyes looked with mascara,
The way my legs felt smooth to the touch,
The way I felt unapologetically myself,
And nobody could take that from me.

But I had to keep it a secret.
It was too much for some people to handle.

They thought I should be a real man,
Be a provider, protector, breadwinner,
The cuddler, the kisser, the initiator,
Even those who said they understood,
Appreciated the dynamic,
Thought it was kinda hot,
Always defaulted to the traditional expectation.
Too emotional, too needy, too affectionate,
"Stop trying to be the little spoon!"
"Stop being scared at loud noises!"
"Stop wearing such bright colors!"
"Stop skipping, stop dancing, stop singing,
Stop wearing eyeliner, stop tilting your head,
Stop putting your hand on your hip,
Stop being so…
Girly!"

Growing up pretending to be a boy,
Girly was the worst thing you could be.
You play like a girl, you cry like a girl,
You were a pussy if you were weak,
You were a girlfriend if you didn't like guns,
Girls couldn't rape guys because,
Huh-huh, you can't rape the willing, LOL, right?
Hey baby, you don't need the gun!
High-five, bro!

I craved to be protected.
I adored feeling like people wanted
To stand up for me
To let me cry
To let them be there for me,
But I couldn't.
I wasn't being honest with myself

Because I was scared.
Terrified.
What would the world think?
What would my parents think?
What would happen to me?
Would I be bullied?
Beaten?
Assaulted?
Killed?

Then I found the Queer Dictionary.
I read through the words, the labels, the definitions.
I wasn't a drag queen.
I wasn't a crossdresser.
Transgender though, that seemed right.
But it was too much commitment.
So I went with gender queer,
Non-binary,
Genderfluid,
Gender nonconforming...
Anything that allowed me to be Marissa,
But not take the full jump.
No hormones, no shots, no meds,
Nothing permanent.
Permanent was scary.

However, as I became Marissa,
I stopped liking being called sir.
I began to hate my deadname.
I began to hate being associated as a guy,
A male,
A him,
A dude,
A bro,

Thank you very much, sir.
Have a nice day, sir.
Is this your husband?
Is this your father?

I wanted to be one of the girls.
I wanted to be a girl.
I... am a girl.
I couldn't even commit to it when I went on HRT,
But my spouse referred to me as Marissa,
Ris,
Rissy Monster,
Princess,
Baby.
He called me beautiful, precious,
Pretty, princess, baby girl...
All the things I wanted to be called my entire life,
But wasn't allowed.
Cause that'd be gay, right?

But then...
Then two people took from me.
Like thieves in the night, they stole.
They took my body.
They took my rights.
They took my voice.
They took
My consent.
I hid.
I ran.
I fled.
I became numb.
Distant.
Vacant.

I cut my hair.
Ditched outfits.
Tossed aside the makeup.
Died inside everytime someone called me Alex,
But I dealt with it.
Because that's what the world was like
To people like me
If I was true.

Then one day, he came to our school.
Pastor Carl.
Filled with hate,
Bigotry,
Moral superiority,
Slurs,
Threats,
Damnation,
Scare-tactics,
Humiliation,
And self-righteousness.
He called girls sluts,
Gay people words I won't repeat,
And trans acceptance was the reason
Penn had a suicide problem.
Not because of bullies like him,
But because being who we are
Was subconscious defiance of truth.
That's why we hurt,
That's why we suffered,
That's why we died,
Because Pastor Carl knew the truth
And we ran from it.
We only chose to be who we were
To mock God.

As I stood up to him,
I was no longer afraid.
Nothing he said could touch me.
Nothing he said could penetrate my shield.
Nothing he said mattered.
So I yelled directly in his face:
"I'm transgender, fuck you!"
And that was it.
I was out.
I was Marissa.

Then we got a new President,
And all hell broke loose.
The same fear I'd had for years,
Seemed to consume the many.
So I wrote,
Yelled,
Podcasted,
Published,
Guested,
Stood up,
Stood out,
Owned who I was,
And within three months,
I was Marissa fuckin' McCool.
Published author,
LGBT columnist,
Trans-podcaster,
Guest on God Awful Movies,
And now, performing in the Vagina Monologues.
As me.
As Marissa.
As Marissa Alexa McCool.

Who I've always been.
True.

Tonight is not my first, or even hundredth
Time on stage in public,
But it is the first time,
The very first time,
That any cast list or program
Will read: Marissa Alexa McCool.
And that, my dear friends,
Was worth every step of the journey.

To Relate is to Humanize

It would be very nice if we weren't all beings that needed to experience something personal before it perhaps changes their mind about something. It's not an uncommon occurrence for transpeople to be the first ones that someone knew who was trans (that they know of.)

A fellow podcaster, and someone quickly becoming a good friend of mine, Felicia from Utah Outcasts, was talking to me about how hard it may be to understand what it's like. Even with her being an ally, supporter, and friend, she still struggles with the direct empathy, and our following conversation helped with that. I only named her because she specifically asked me to.

I decided to write about this because, for some reason, I'm usually able to put something in my head into a context that most people can accept, or at least understand. Maybe it's all the years on camera, writing, and performing, or just something at which I'm naturally adept, but either way, I'm glad I can do this because it helps put a human face on this issue. For so many transpeople, they are demonized by people they've never met and have no idea what the personal experience is like (Fuck you, Milo.) It wasn't until gay people were humanized for a majority of the population that the swift social change took place, taking us from re-electing GW because of catching the gay, and marriage equality becoming national law eleven years later.She was open, but thought she could never really "get" it.

I started off by asking her a question. In situations like this, it's always important for an open-ended inquiry that gauges someone's common experience so that the gap can be bridged. It's far harder to do with someone hostile, but it still holds true. We are more easily accepting of similarities than differences as a species. Given her experience and position at which she arrived in podcasting, I basically asked if there had ever been anything she'd done where she knew it was the right thing and it was her decision to make, but people rejected her for it, to the point of believing they knew better than you, for religious or any other reason.

Felicia opened up about her divorce and how she was pretty much on her own handling it. She had family side with the other, and was told repeatedly how there is no divorce in the eyes of God. Marriage is forever. Divorce is a sin. She had a very difficult journey through people who are supposed to love her no matter what treating her that way.

Then I said, "Okay, now imagine you were born into that marriage, but you never wanted to be married in the first place, and you still got that reaction. Imagine everyone felt the right to tell you that you were born unhappilly married and even though you'll get divorced, you're really still married. It's a dismissal of your identity, of your personhood, of other people telling you that they have more of a right to define who you are than you do.

That's the point where she brought up there being no divorce in the eyes of God, according to those accosting her. I related to that too, because I get told

---

63

God doesn't make mistakes which is why my gender identity can't possibly be legitimate or valid.

I feel like the next part of the exchange can only be quoted instead of summarized, simply because I couldn't possibly say it any better than it went down between the two of us.

FELICIA: For me it was like digging my way out from my own grave, and there were those who told me the grave was were I was supposed to be. Trying to push me out. And no matter how much they hurt me, or how much they said I was wrong, I'd seen the sky and I couldn't go back in the grave.

MARISSA: Yes. That is what it was like the first time someone called me a girl, called me Marissa. I couldn't pretend it wasn't anymore.

FELICIA: And you had seen inside yourself and you liked what you saw there.

MARISSA: I knew it was right. Correct. Who I really was.No matter who said it wasn't so.

FELICIA: And the overwhelming joy despite the pain of what others did meant I had to keep going.There's wasn't a choice anymore.

This. This. So much this. Maybe I shouldn't have to do this, but this is why I make myself so open and available, because many transpeople are not in a place where they can or are able to do that themselves. But the only way it's going to become more reasonable in society as a whole is if there is a human face on it beyond Caitlyn Jenner's. Our sense of empathy is more strongly provoked by being able to know someone, see it for yourself, and understand that experience. I've been on the other side of that equation for many things, and hopefully we can progress beyond needing to do that someday.

For now, I just thought this was a pretty damn cool exchange, and I'm grateful that Felicia let me talk about it to all of you.

Prone

I probably don't even need to add anything to that word for you to know what I mean. Especially being a person of the LGBT community, we know to what it connects.

For the last four years, I've attended a university with a suicide epidemic. Last count, I believe, was 13 kids have commited suicide at our University since 2013, when I started attending. There are those who argue that comparatively, this is not a large number of people, given the size of our campus. I would say to those people that one person committing suicide is too many.

Yeah, this post isn't going to be friendly to the apologetics crowd.

The suicide rate, as well as rates for depression, anxiety, and self-destructive behavior has shown to be higher among those of the LGBT community. This, unfortunately, gives people like Milo and Pastor Carl all the evidence they need to throw at us, to tell us how wrong we are. It's obviously happening because we know we're wrong with God, so that's why we end up so depressed, right?

Fuck you, Carl. Both of you.

I went on a rant about this on the episode of *God Awful Movies* (#73) on which I was a guest, but it needs to be said; more often, louder, and directly at those who use this as fodder to bully LGBT kids at universities.

Maybe those kids get depressed because people like you advocate for their bullying. Maybe those kids get depressed because you're in their face, constantly using your so-called loving God to threaten them with lakes of fire and hatred. Maybe those kids are constantly looking over their shoulder because you elected a narcisstic fuckwit who has emboldened those with hatred in their hearts, and has given those people the idea that consequence-free hate speech is and should be a thing.

I go to a school that has trans-inclusive healthcare, an LGBT Center, and an entire system that allowed me to change my name simply by identifying as transgender, but do not think for a solitary second that I've taken that for granted. I know I'm one of the lucky ones. I've read my email inbox. I know how many people can't even be themselves in their own home, let alone at school, or anywhere else. Somehow, even with bullying being demonized and preached against, when it comes to us, it's given a free-pass... or at least it's treated less seriously.

Back when I was a kid, and people wrongfully assumed that I was gay, I was tortured. TORTURED. on a daily basis. Rarely did anyone even stop to lend a hand, let alone step in to help or do something about it. The school wrote me off as a misanthropic fuck-up, and those who perpetrated my daily hazing only got more emboldened as they saw no consequence whatsoever for their behavior.

16 years later, I watch as even on a "liberal Ivy League safe-space loving LGBT-supporting campus," for the

most part I just deal with the long, awkward stares and the jokes under their breath of which they think I'm unaware. Don't get me wrong, I have a great circle of friends there and I wouldn't trade them for anything, but even if I know 25 people, that's less than one percent of the student body. That may go up with an article being published in the *Daily Pennsylvanian* about my book, but the bottom line is that even some of the most open-minded people don't get what transgender is, don't care to, and/or leave that out of their "love trumps hate" platform.

That's what people like Milo love to exploit: Set people against each other and pick on what is perceived as the most vulnerable among us.

And when people stand up to him, he cancels his appearance and blames protestors, because he'd rather pretend to be a victim than face someone he can't destroy with his words. He runs a segment called "How to Spot a Tranny" but if people protest him, it hurts his feelings. He puts targets on the back of vulnerable young kids, and our President wants to remove Federal funding for people who don't want this hate speech on their campus.

This is what it's come to. Our President hires people who deliver hate speech, supports people who spout it and put vulnerable kids in danger, and then complain when others stand up for them.

Because bullies love nothing more than someone different and weak going home and crying. Or worse, committing suicide.

—

As Pastor Carl said, "those kids killed themselves because they were ashamed." When you can use the statistics of a suicide rate on campus to justify pointing out the queer kids so that you can threaten them, bully them into suicide, or break their heart, that is the behavior that's being endorsed by the President of the United States. Quick though, better allow us to be discriminated against because of "sincerely-held religious beliefs." Wouldn't want our existence to interfere with someone's bigotry.

Can I discriminate against someone being a dick? At my old retail job, can I refuse to serve someone because I don't like their attitude? That's against my religion for the sake of this argument. Treating people that serve you as if they're below you, that's against my sincerely-held religious belief that you should go fuck yourself, so are we allowed to refuse service based on our religious belief? Or are you only allowed to discriminate against queers? And is it only allowed to be under one religion? You know, the persecuted one that now has almost blanket representation in our country... again.

So I'm sorry if I've been yelling about this too much, but at the same time, I need to keep doing so before this becomes normalized again, because I refuse to go back to immediate post-9/11 conservative times where anyone who wasn't a mindless straight Christian patriot was demonized and called un-American. I thought we were over that bullshit.

But if I've learned anything, it's that anytime we truly believe we've found the bottom as to how low these people will stoop, they find the trap door button and prove us wrong yet again. Congratulations, fuckwits, you did it once more!

It's All in the Feelings

The election cycle of 2016 was a unique one among all its predecessors. A non-politician ran for President, breaking every rule in the book of political correctness and polite society, and still ended up winning despite the minority of the votes by a few million. Supporters of Donald Trump were particularly vicious in their "Make American Great Again!" slogan, while detractors were equally as emotionally opposed to the views brought forth by the Republican candidate, now President-elect. It's no secret that America has been cast as polarized and tense; the country fought a Civil War over it 150 years ago, so what is it about this particular election cycle and rhetoric that increased our vigor and vitriol? Why are people so divided by controversial topics, religion, and politics? And, if we have those answers, what can we do about trying to bridge those gaps that were set ablaze with differing opinions and perspectives? This paper will demonstrate both the identities of the cause and solutions for what can be done to help the very issue of political divisiveness.

Political divisiveness and polarization are not new to discourse, even within our own country. In fact, it's very likely that those traits were developed selectively through evolution. As evolution can be the survival and reproduction of the fittest physically, those with certain mental mindsets and intuitions could just as well be a selective trait in the modern day human society. *Homo sapien* is a social creature, and part of being social is forming a community. These communities range in size from small groups of nomadic bands to cities in the millions. Therefore, it stands to reason that the intuitive feeling of finding something in common with a fellow human being, while also being unified by characteristics that are different from the other goes back to the very beginning of modern human civilization.

Dr. Jonathan Haidt describes these feelings as intuitionism in his book *The Righteous Mind: How Good People Are Divided by Politics and Religion*. He describes how our feelings are triggered, "We make our first judgments rapidly, and we are dreadful at seeking out evidence that might disconfirm those initial judgments. Yet friends can do for us what we cannot for ourselves: they can challenge us, giving us reasons and arguments that sometime trigger new intuitions, thereby making it possible for us to change our minds. (Haidt 2012, p. 55)" Social experiments have been conducted show that when placed in an environment, humans are innately tribal, in that they both form communities and work together based on common goals, and also get intuitively defensive and aggressive toward other groups simultaneously.

"It now appears that warfare has been a constant feature of human life since long before agriculture and private property," Haidt explains. "For millions of years, therefore, our ancestors faced the adaptive challenge of forming and maintaining coalitions that could fend off challenges and attacks from rival groups. We are the descendants of successful tribalists, not their more individualistic cousins. (Haidt 2012, p. 163)" The reason for this is that those who were loners were much more likely to get killed by a rival tribe or a natural predator, but those who formed those coalitions and groups could withstand the attack. Our ancestors forged common bonds with each other to survive, and socialization and cooperation between groups of people became selective in an evolutionary sense. It also created tension with others who weren't part of that group, and the groups of humans could organize against those differences in an effort to unify themselves based on commonalities.

Religion is very much the same way; it harkens back to our need to be a part of something greater than ourselves. Haidt uses the example of attending a college football game to demonstrate these effects, showing how they are unified for a common cause. They aren't there just for the game, but they gather in similar areas beforehand, socializing and bonding. They dress in similar colors and then march to the stadium, where they collectively know what to sing, what to yell, and who to hate. "Why do the students sing, chant, dance, sway, chop, and stomp so enthusiastically during the game? Showing support for their football team may help to motivate the players, but is that the function of these behaviors? Are they done in order to achieve victory?" While that may be the conscious idea, it runs much deeper than that, and that's where the intuitionism comes into play. "A college football game is a superb analogy for religion. From a naïve perspective, focusing only on what is most visible... college football is an extravagant, costly, wasteful institution that impairs people's ability to think rationally... But from a sociologically informed perspective, it is a religious rite that does just what it is supposed to do: it pulls people up from Durkheim's lower level (the profane) to his higher level (the sacred).

It flips the hive switch and makes people feel, for a few hours, that they are 'simply a part of a whole.' (Haidt 2012, p. 287-88)

Being a part of a bigger whole, something greater than yourself, is a fundamental core of almost, if not all, religions. Since there are different religions across the board, it's similar to Haidt's metaphor of college football, where different tribes do battle against each other with a single, unified goal: winning the war (game). Tensions are difficult to work through in this scenario because that's not the goal, and it's intuitive to see the Other as the enemy. Whereas a single person might be rational in discussing alliances with someone from a different team, being part of those thousands of people taps into a completely emotional force, which is much more difficult to rationalize. Therefore, it would make sense that our views of religion are very similar.

Moral Psychology has done a great deal of research in this area so answers can be found at times of seemingly-extreme polarization, and 2016 is no exception. Sam Harris also researches this question of religious divisiveness in his book *The Moral Landscape*. "The question of whether religion (or anything else) might have given groups of human beings an evolutionary advantage (so-called 'group selection') has been widely debated. And even if tribes have occasionally been the vehicles of natural selection, and religion proved adaptive, it would remain an open question whether religion increases human fitness today... There are a wide variety of genetically entrenched human traits (e.g., out-group aggression, infidelity, superstition, etc.) that, while probably adaptive at some point in our past, may have been less than optimal even in the Pleistoscene. In a world that is growing ever more crowded and complex, many of these biologically selected traits may yet imperil us. (Harris 2010, p. 148)"

Bringing about these traits being adaptive then puts people in the position of wondering what they can do about it. After all, if it's all emotional and not rational, doesn't that mean that it's natural, and therefore nothing can be done about it? Of course not. As demonstrated by Harris, it doesn't matter if it was a selective advantage; it isn't now, and by being aware of that, we can move past the instinct to fight anyone who might be different. It's hard to argue that unifying against an Other without having a rational or logical reason to do so is good for society. Commenting on this social evolution, albeit while explaining a different principal, Noam Chomsky dissects this idea and questions not if it's harmful, but how harmful it could be. "Still more remote are the fundamental questions that motivated the classical theory of mind – the creative aspect of language use, the distinction between action appropriate to situations and action caused by situations, between being 'compelled' to act in certain ways or 'incited and inclined to do so.' (Chomsky 2002, p. 61-91)" What stands to reason here is that the sociological effects of these instincts may have caused early humans to selectively develop that trait, but being at a time and age where those distinctions can be made is essential to figuring out how they can be solved.

Once it's established that religious and political divisiveness is inherently natural, intuitive, and emotional, that brings us to practical solutions. It must, however, start not only with acknowledgement of human evolution being a scientific fact, but that it doesn't stop. Having a past trait does not necessarily mean it will be the one that's passed on, and if the conscious choice is made to work through this intuitiveness, then that will be the trait that transcends generations as it did for our ancestors. "We cannot step away from evolution," Bill Nye argues in *Undeniable*. "Our genomes are always collecting mutations, and we are always making mate selections. Are humans preferentially mating with other humans who are tall" Blonde or not blonde? Sweet, or bitches and jerks? With all of our glamor magazines and self-help books, are we solely producing offspring who are smarter and better-looking? … I can't help wondering if that is part of the selection effect. (Nye 2014. P. 262)"

The first step toward fixing a problem is admitting there is one, and with the great intelligence of humankind, polarization within countries and communities is a large one. Therefore, by pointing it out and acknowledging it, humans can work toward making the world less polarized by stepping back from themselves and reconsidering what their instinct tells them to do and how they emotionally react. Nye's explanation of continuous evolution shows that it can be done, and if humans learn to react with empathy rather than defensiveness, that will become an innate trait in future humanity. Asking why one person reacted that way to something one said, rather than attacking them because they said something that's of a different perspective, leads to learning, empathy for others, and one less fight in the world. If that can be done on an individual level, it will become a selective trait. The awareness of its existence provides the opportunity to change it, and gives people the advice to step back when they feel emotionally charged over something divisive. Once that step is taken back, empathy for another human may allow them to go beyond their first instinct and find out something about the other person, and in turn themselves, the same way enthnographic anthropologists have been doing for years. Or, as Noam Chomsky put it in his interview with me, "Become seriously engaged in things that matter (sic), ranging from research and education to organizing and activism... Which is not new. That's how it has always been, and thanks to those who decided to care and act, over time it has often become a better world. Same in the future. (Chomsky 2016)"

Dr. Chomsky is correct in asserting that it isn't new, as can be evidenced by writings from hundreds of years ago. In regard to religion in society, Immanuel Kant had many of the same sentiments toward religion and the application of reason. "More modern, though far less prevalent, is the contrasted optimistic belief, which indeed has gained a following solely among philosophers, and, of late, especially among those interested in education – the belief that the world steadily (though almost imperceptibly) forges in the other direction, to wit, from bad to better; at least that the predisposition to such a movement is discoverable in human nature. If this belief, however, is meant to apply to moral goodness and badness (not simply to the process of civilization), it has certainly not been deduced from experience; the history of all times cries too loudly against it. The belief, we may presume, is a well-intended assumption of the moralists, from Seneca to Rousseau, designed to encourage the sedulous cultivation of that seed of goodness which perhaps lies in us – if indeed, we can count on any such natural basis of goodness in man. We may not that since we take for granted that man is by nature sound of body (as of birth he usually is), no reason appears why, by nature, his soul should not be deemed similarly healthy and free from evil. Is not nature herself, then, inclined to lend her aid to developing in this moral predisposition in goodness? (Kant 1794, p. 370)" This writing from Kant predates Darwin's voyage, and yet bears that all-important truth upon which we can build: we can count on the fact that humans can be inherently good, and there's no reason why they shouldn't be.

If human beings can discern that being divided by politics and/or religion is inherently bad for the future of the species, they can start working toward ways to work past those intuitive biases. Acknowledging our own and reaching out to others not only develops empathy, but makes one naturally more relativist in their mindset. In the age of nuclear weapons and instant military action, preventing mass destruction will rely upon the majority of the human race coming to the decision that everyone is equally human, and in the words of Bill Pullman in *Independence Day*, "we cannot be consumed by our petty differences anymore. (*Independence Day*, 1996)" Let's not let it come to the end of the world before making that realization.

In summary, humans being divided by religion and politics is a product of intuitionism being a selective trait in the social being they are. With this knowledge and the ability to step back and rationalize, rhetoric and the quality of life between peoples of all different kinds can be immensely improved. Philosophers and scientists of many varying fields have come to similar conclusions about the problem, the symptoms, and at least somewhat sure of a solution. It will take a long time, it won't be easy for many people, but working past that which was once selective is what brought the world our modern civilizations as they are. If humans can survive those, they can survive learning to recognize when they've acted and reacted emotionally, and compel themselves to consider alternate perspectives with empathy and relativism. Perhaps this knowledge can bring about one solitary evolutionary trait: the future human society having the social bonding power with all humans, regardless of origin, race, or any other characteristic. Humanity has the ability to accomplish this, but the question will be if they also have the willpower to do so.

Works Cited

Chomsky, Noam. Personal Interview. September 30th, 2016. Email.

Chomsky, Noam. *On Nature and Language*, ed. Adrianna Belletti and Luiigi Rizzi. Cambridge University Press, 2002. Compilation.

Emmerich, Roland. *Independence Day*. 20th Century Fox. 1996. Film.

Haidt, Jonathan. *The Righteous Mind: Why Good People Are Divided by Politics and Religion*. Vintage Books. 2012. Book.

Harris, Sam. *The Moral Landscape: How Science Can Determine Human Values.* Free Press. 2010. Book.

Kant, Immanuel. *Basic Writings of Kant.* Edited and with an introduction by Allen W. Wood. Modern Library. 2001. Book.

Nye, Bill. *Undeniable: Evolution and the Science of Creation.* St. Martin's Griffin. 2014.

Made in the USA
Columbia, SC
19 December 2018